FUN FACTS ABOUT
Farm
Equipment

Written by
Ray H. Miller

Illustrated by
Andrew Crabtree

The ERTL Company, Inc. would like to thank the following companies who helped make Fun Facts About Farm Equipment possible:

AGCO Corporation; Babson Bros. Co.; Case Corporation; Chore-Time Equipment; Corel Corporation; Deere & Company; Farm Safety 4 Just Kids; Melroe Company; New Holland North America, Inc.; and Reinke Manufacturing Co. Inc.

PHOTO CREDITS

AGCO CORPORATION

Page 7 photo of Model 9650 courtesy of AGCO Corporation.
Page 19 photo of GLEANER® Model R72 courtesy of AGCO Corporation.

BABSON BROS. CO.

Page 23 photo of Surge Auto Flow™ courtesy of Babson Bros.

CASE CORPORATION

Page 9 photo of Model 3900 courtesy of Case Corporation.
Page 21 photo of Model 8465 courtesy of Case Corporation.

CHORE-TIME EQUIPMENT

Page 25 photo of Model H2™ Feeder courtesy of Chore-Time Equipment.
Page 27 photo of bulk feed storage tank courtesy of Chore-Time Equipment.

COREL PROFESSIONAL PHOTOGRAPHS

Page 5 photo of barn courtesy of Corel.
Page 29 photo of silos courtesy of Corel.

JOHN DEERE

Cover photo of Model 8960 courtesy of Deere & Company.
Page 11 photo of MaxEmerge planter courtesy of Deere & Company.

MELROE COMPANY

Page 13 photo of Model 3630 Spra-Coupe® sprayer courtesy of Melroe Company.

NEW HOLLAND NORTH AMERICA, INC.

Page 17 photo of tractor Model 4230 and the Braud 524 grape harvester from New Holland courtesy of New Holland North America, Inc.

REINKE MANUFACTURING CO.

Page 15 photo of Canal-fed Lateral Move Maxigator courtesy of Reinke Manufacturing Co.

Printed in the U.S.A.
ISBN 1-887327-00-2
10 9 8 7 6 5 4 3 2 1

TABLE OF CONTENTS

Down on the Farm	4
Tractors	6
Plows	8
Planters	10
Spreaders	12
Irrigation	14
Harvesters	16
Combines	18
Hay Balers	20
Dairy Systems	22
Feeders	24
Bulk Tanks	26
Silos	28
Quitting Time	30
Safety Tips	31

DOWN ON THE FARM

Fun Facts About Farm Equipment will show you a side of farm equipment you've never seen. This book takes a look at some ordinary farm equipment with some extraordinary characteristics. Whether they're tractors, combines, or fruit pickers, you'll find out that there's more to equipment than turning a key, pressing a button, or shifting a gear.

Why would a farmer need a machine with the suction power of 30 vacuum cleaners? Who spent four-and-a-half months behind the wheel of a tractor? How many bushels of hay would you have to stack to reach the top of the Empire State Building? Keep turning the pages of *Fun Facts About Farm Equipment* to find out the answers to these questions, and much, much more.

TRACTORS

One of the most important parts of a farm is the hard-working tractor. Whether it's plowing, planting, or cultivating, the tractor pulls a heavy load on today's farm. Because tractors are used for so many things, they are usually very big and powerful. Some even have cabs (where the driver sits) with air conditioners and heaters. Gear down and read these interesting facts about tractors.

COMPACTOR TRACTOR

The largest tractor in the world is the U.S. Department of Agriculture Wide Tractive Frame Vehicle. It weighs 24.5 tons and measures 33 feet from wheel to wheel. You could park 6 compact cars side by side between the wheels of this amazing tractor.

TRACTOR TRAVELERS

Can you imagine traveling 14,500 miles behind the wheel of a tractor? The Young Farmers Group of Devon, Great Britain, can.

They left Devon on October 18, 1990, and drove their tractor and a supporting trailor all the way to Zimbabwe, Africa, arriving there on March 4, 1991. That would be like driving from New York to Los Angeles almost six times.

NEED A LIFT?

The Deutz-Allis 9100 Series tractor can lift nearly 10,000 pounds, or 5 tons. A tractor that powerful could lift 8 cows, 3 ponies, 15 goats, and 10 chickens. And if there were any room left, it could even add on a dog and 2 cats.

TRACTOR TIME!

Modern tractors like the AGCO ALLIS 9650 have come a very long way from those used on farms in the late 1800's. Back then, they were called *traction engines*. These large, heavy tractors had steel wheels instead of rubber tires and were powered by steam, not gasoline. They were so powerful, they could pull nearly 40 plows at one time! Today's tractors may not have the "muscle" of the old traction engines, but they are much easier to maneuver and they have radios, air-conditioned cabs, and passenger seats.

PLOWS

The plow is a basic tractor attachment. It is one of the most important pieces of equipment on the farm, because it is used to prepare the soil for growing crops. A popular plow is the *moldboard plow*. It digs, or tills, the soil so air and water can keep it fertile. Another type of plow is the *disk plow*. It has round blades that till hard soil. A *cultivator* is similar to a plow. It loosens the soil and digs out weeds. Let's "dig" up more facts about plows and cultivators.

ROLLING TEETH
The 12-Row Lilliston Rolling® Cultivator really "chews" up the soil it plows. It has a 12-row rotary bottom. Each row contains a group of five rotors, and each rotor has a set of ten teeth.

With 600 teeth in all, there are more teeth on this cultivator than there are in a group of 20 adults.

PLOWED UNDER
Some farmers use a plow called a "ditcher" to dig ditches for irrigation, so water can flow onto their fields. The Maletti

Mod.2G 130 can dig ditches 50 inches deep. You could place 14 medium-sized apples on top of each other in a ditch that deep, and the apple on top would be level with the ground.

FOUR-LANE...FIELD?
Someone should put a sign saying "wide load" on the back of the 4900 Vibra Shank® from Case International.

This super-wide cultivator is over 50 feet in width from side to side.

That's about as wide as a four-lane highway.

POWER PLOWERS

A farmer looking to buy a plow like the 3900 Tandem Disk Harrow by Case International can visit a modern showroom where they'll find catalogs that have important information about plows. In the old days, farm-equipment makers thought of different ways to promote their equipment. One way was to hold plowing contests in large fields where hundreds of farmers gathered to watch. The winning tractor-plow combination earned a gold medal, but more importantly it was known for being the best equipment in the business.

PLANTERS

Once the soil has been plowed, it's time to plant the crops. Farmers accomplish this by using planters. There are many types of planters available, such as corn, wheat, and soybean planters. Most planters are basically the same, however. Each has a *tank* to hold the seeds, a *feed meter* to drop the right amount of seeds, and a row of *wheels* to cover the seeds with soil. Plant yourself down and read these amazing facts about planters.

PRECISION PLANTING

The vegetable planter by SK Design has a vacuum drum that pulls individual seeds through tiny holes in the drum and deposits each onto a precise spot in a tray. This amazing planter can plant up to 392,000 seeds in one hour. That many seeds could produce enough lettuce to make one bowl of salad for everyone living in the state of West Virginia.

COURTSIDE SEEDS

The Case International 8500 Air Hoe Drill is one wide planter! It wouldn't be stretching

it to say this planter is nearly as wide as the baseline of a basketball court. It can plant seeds in 77 rows at one time.

GARDENS OF SALAD

Hungry for a salad? You could plant all the ingredients – lettuce, spinach, carrots, cucumbers, celery, onions, radishes, beets, and tomato seeds – with the Stanhay Singulaire 785. Most planters can plant one or two types of crops. Using special seed disks, this machine can plant more than 40 different kinds of seeds, even watermelon seeds.

DOUBLE THE PLANTER

Planters like the John Deere MaxEmerge planter (pictured above) are very important machines to the farmer. For a planter that does twice the work, consider another John Deere planter: the 455 Folding Drill, a high-tech planter that is 35 feet wide. Farmers can fold the two 12½ foot outer wing units together, and they have a planter that is only 15 feet wide. It's easier to store that way, but more importantly, farmers don't have to worry about knocking over stop signs when they're driving along rural roads back to the barn.

SPREADERS

Once the crops are planted, farmers use spreaders to spread fertilizers to help the plants grow. These heavy-duty machines are pulled by a tractor and can spread tons of manure, lime, pot ash, and other types of fertilizers. Machines which spread liquid chemicals to reduce weeds and insects are called *sprayers*. Most sprayers have *booms*, or mechanical arms that spray crops. Let's see what facts "crop up" about spreaders and sprayers.

UP...UP...AND A-SPRAY!

The Big A sprayer is really big! Its tires are nearly 6 feet tall, and its storage tank holds up to 8 tons of chemicals.

What's most amazing about the Big A is that its boom is 60 feet long. That's 15 feet wider than the wings on a Learjet!

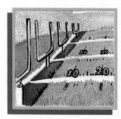

FOOTBALL FERTILIZER

Conibear Equipment Company in Lakeland, Florida, makes a fertilizer spreader that hauls over 5 tons of material at once. Farmers who use this super-sized spreader can fertilize an area the size of 4 football fields before having to go back to the barn and fill up.

INCREDI-SPREADER

Multipurpose spreaders don't just spread fertilizer. These incredible spreaders also plant seeds and spray for weeds and insects. A farmer using a multipurpose spreader can plant, spray, and fertilize 230 acres of potato plants in one day. A farmer using a separate seeder, sprayer, and spreader may finish only 75 acres. That's a difference of over 3 million potato plants.

SPORTY SPRAYER

Caught in a traffic jam? No problem. Climb aboard the 3630 Spra-Coupe® by the Melroe Company. This futuristic four-wheel spraying machine has a 300-gallon liquid tank and a 60-foot boom. Amazingly, it sits 4 feet off the ground, and the front and rear tires are over 10 feet apart. The Spra-Coupe is designed that way so it can ride high over the top of the crops while it is spraying for weeds and insects. With that much clearance, it could also drive right over a sports car without putting a scratch or dent in it.

IRRIGATION

Without water, plants do not grow. In dry climates, farmers use irrigation. The most common system is *surface irrigation*: a series of canals carry water from a source such as a lake to holding ditches, and then eventually to the crops. Where water sources aren't available, farmers use *sprinkler irrigation*. A pump pulls water out of a well and sends it to a sprinkler head located on top of a moving metal tower. Splash into these facts about irrigation.

A LOTTA WATER

Crops that are grown to be made into food need more water than you'd think. Did you know that it takes 115 gallons of water to grow enough wheat to make just one loaf of bread? That's 2,453 glasses of water!

NEED A SHOWER?

Have you ever been sprayed with a hose on a hot summer day?

Try to imagine what it would be like to be sprayed with water from a field irrigation system. Some of the larger irrigation systems can spray water over 400 feet. You could be on one side of the Mississippi River in certain places and soak someone standing on the other side!

GREATER LAKE!

About 40% of all the water used in the U.S. is used for irrigation. Irrigation systems use enough water in one day to fill a lake that is 5 miles long, 1 mile wide, and 130 feet deep.

In one year, that would be enough water to fill Crater Lake, the deepest lake in the U.S., over 6 times.

JUST A SECOND!

There are areas in the U.S. that don't receive enough rain to grow crops. In those areas, some farmers use machines like a canal-fed lateral moving irrigation system to water their crops. It's amazing to think how much water is used for irrigation in the United States. In one day, we use 140 billion gallons of water. In one hour, we use 5.8 billion gallons. And in just one second, we use 1.6 million gallons. In that second, there would be enough water to fill a bathtub for each person living in Annapolis, Maryland's state capital!

HARVESTERS

Harvesters pick the fruits and vegetables grown on farms. Carrot and radish harvesters are *sub soilers*, which go underground and loosen the soil. Above ground, moving belts and pulleys pluck the carrots and radishes out of the soil. Orange pickers have arms that shake the trees, causing the fruit to drop onto cloths. Grape pickers have mechanical arms that pick the fruit from the vine. Here are a few facts about harvesters to pick from.

CARROTS ALL AROUND!

On a good day, Zellwin Farms in Zellwood, Florida, can harvest enough carrots to feed an entire city. The harvester they built themselves can pick 375,000 pounds of carrots in one day. With that many carrots you could give 1 carrot to each person living in the city of Chicago.

EARS AND EARS FOR YEARS AND YEARS

Some corn harvesters can pick about 250,000 ears of corn in one day. To finish that much corn, you would have to eat 2 ears every night for dinner for the next 342 years!

"GOVERNOR, YOUR MARMALADE HAS ARRIVED"

Orange-picking machines are fast workers. In one hour they can pick almost 3,000 oranges. If you made orange marmalade with those oranges, you would have enough of it to give 30 jars to the governor of each state in the U.S., including Alaska and Hawaii.

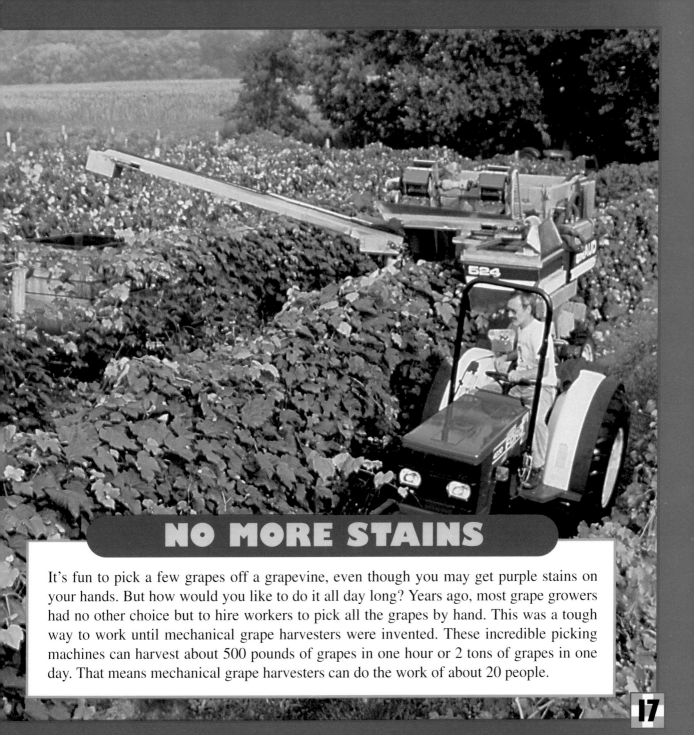

NO MORE STAINS

It's fun to pick a few grapes off a grapevine, even though you may get purple stains on your hands. But how would you like to do it all day long? Years ago, most grape growers had no other choice but to hire workers to pick all the grapes by hand. This was a tough way to work until mechanical grape harvesters were invented. These incredible picking machines can harvest about 500 pounds of grapes in one hour or 2 tons of grapes in one day. That means mechanical grape harvesters can do the work of about 20 people.

COMBINES

One of the largest and most useful machines on a farm is the combine, which looks like a small mobile factory. A wheat combine cuts and cleans the grain. A corn combine picks the corn, husks it, and removes the kernels. Combines have a large tank that stores the crop. When the tank is full, the crop is unloaded through a long arm, called an *auger*, and onto a truck or wagon beside it. Take a load off and read these facts about combines.

"GENTLEMEN, START YOUR COMBINES"

No one will ever confuse the New Holland TR combine with a race car – especially when its average speed while cutting wheat is only 2 mph. By the time this combine could make one lap at the Indianapolis 500, a race car would pass it 64 times.

NO HORSING AROUND

It takes a mighty big engine to run a combine. Not only does the engine run the huge rotating blades that cut the crop, it also powers the conveyors and the elevator. That's why some combines have a 330-horsepower engine. It would take 27 riding lawn mowers to equal the power in this terrific wheat trimmer.

TWO IN ONE

Combines are probably the largest movable machinery on the farm.

An average combine is 25 feet long. Grain that enters the combine is carried along a twisting, turning, zigzagging conveyor that runs inside the combine. From the time it enters until the time it is emptied into a truck, the grain travels about 50 feet. That's twice the length of the combine.

MECHANICAL HORSE

Driving combines like the GLEANER® R72 is nothing like it was in the late 1800's. Modern combines have hydraulic (liquid-moved) systems that give the driver power steering for safe and easy handling. There are switches to raise and lower the platform, and buttons to change the thresher speed from slow to fast. Early combines didn't even have engines. They did, however, have a lot of "horsepower." In 1880 a combine was pulled by a team of 33 mules. It must have been a real chore just to start up that combine!

HAY BALERS

The large, round bales of hay that sit in the farm fields are made by hay balers. There are two kinds of hay balers: *round balers* and *square balers*. These balers rake the hay or straw inside the baler, pack it together, wrap twine around the bale, then drop them out the back. Some smaller square balers throw the bales into a wagon being pulled by a tractor. Don't "bale out" before you read these facts about hay balers.

EMPIRE STATE BALE-DING

The Case International 8580 baler makes big bales. These bales measure up to 9 feet long and weigh up to 2,200 pounds! In one day it can make 250 bales. If all those bales could be stacked on top of each other end to end, they would be almost twice as tall as the Empire State Building in New York City.

NOTHING BUT NET

The state of Indiana is probably best known for its basketball, but it is also

known for its hay baling. If the amount of twine one baler can hold was turned into basketball nets, there would be enough to supply over 2,000 basketball courts in Indiana with 2 nets each.

WORTH ITS WEIGHT

Many farmers feel hay balers are worth their weight in gold. Some balers can bale 1,000 pounds of hay in less than 1 minute. If balers really were worth their weight in gold, a New Idea 4865 baler would be worth almost $20 million.

BALING BONANZA

In the early 1900's, before the invention of the hay baler, a team of horses and farmers would cut and rake the hay out in the fields. Then they would haul wagon loads of it back to the barn for storage. This would usually take them a full day just to finish one acre. With the use of a modern baler like the Case International 8465 round baler, farmers can bale 45 acres of hay, and make 100 bales a day. Some small square balers can produce up to 2,500 bales a day! These machines really "bail" farmers out of a lot of hard work.

DAIRY SYSTEMS

On a dairy farm, farmers use machines to collect the milk and eggs. A *milking machine* is a suction system that pumps milk from the cow to a pipe that feeds into a bulk milk cooler. To gather eggs in the laying house, poultry farmers use *conveyor belts* that run beneath the cage. Eggs roll out of the cage onto the conveyor belt which carries them to a central egg collection house. Let's "egg-zamine" dairy systems in a little more detail.

SUPER SUCTION

The Westfalia Systemat RDP-40 is a high-powered vacuum pump that can milk many cows at once. The suction from the RDP-40 is about the same as the suction from 32 household vacuum cleaners combined. If you could use this vacuum to clean the house, you'd probably pick up a lot more than dirt!

HAVE SOME EGGNOG, SANTA!

Conveyor belts used in chicken farms run constantly in order to carry as many eggs into the collection house as possible. Some conveyors can carry enough eggs to make over 3,000 gallons of eggnog a day. That's enough to give Santa Claus a glass of eggnog in every shopping mall he visits in the U.S.

MEGA-MOO-MILK

A milking machine makes life easier for the dairy farmer. It also helps them produce an amazing amount of milk. These incredible machines can milk over 30 cows at a time and produce about 165 gallons of milk a day. That's enough to give 1 glass of milk to every professional football player.

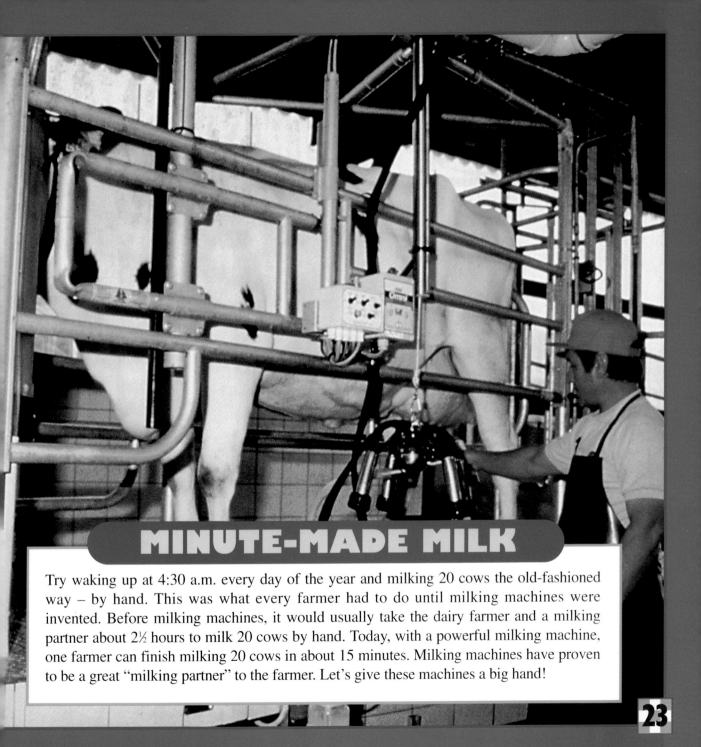

MINUTE-MADE MILK

Try waking up at 4:30 a.m. every day of the year and milking 20 cows the old-fashioned way – by hand. This was what every farmer had to do until milking machines were invented. Before milking machines, it would usually take the dairy farmer and a milking partner about 2½ hours to milk 20 cows by hand. Today, with a powerful milking machine, one farmer can finish milking 20 cows in about 15 minutes. Milking machines have proven to be a great "milking partner" to the farmer. Let's give these machines a big hand!

FEEDERS

If there's one thing farm animals love to do, it's eat. Luckily there are machines that take care of feeding the animals at meal time. Modern farms have equipment that mixes the feed and sends it on a conveyer into the feeding troughs for the animals to eat. When an animal gets thirsty, it simply presses its nose onto a lever inside a water trough and it gets a drink of cold, refreshing water. Fill yourself up on these fantastic feeder fun facts.

MIXER MANIA
The grain-O-vator is a machine that mixes the feed before it is given to the animals. Large feed mixers can weigh up to two tons when they are full. It would take 200 household mixers filled with chocolate chip cookie dough just to equal the weight of that monster mixer.

LET'S EAT!
Cows are big eaters, so it's a good thing there are conveyor belts to help with feeding.

On some medium-sized farms, one conveyor can carry 1.5 tons of feed to the feeding troughs at meal time. That's about the weight of 4,000 T.V. dinners!

WATER LOGGED
The next time you stop by a water fountain, imagine drinking from it non-stop for an hour and 10 minutes. In that amount of time you would have drank the same amount of water a cow drinks from a water trough in one day.

FEEDING TIME

Feeding chickens must have been a real chore before automatic feeding systems came along. Farmers used to have to feed the chickens by hand, but automatic feeders have made chicken feeding much easier. Some feeders have small plastic windows that open automatically to let the feed fill into the pan. They also have a large center dome that causes chickens to eat near the outer edges, which makes it a more comfortable place to eat. With automatic feeders, farmers and their chickens are much happier these days!

BULK TANKS

Farmers store their crops in bulk tanks to keep them fresh. *Bulk milk coolers* come in different shapes and sizes, but they are all designed to keep the milk cold until it goes to a dairy company. *Corn cribs* are usually large structures that are made of metal wire or wood. *Grain tanks* are huge metal tanks that store large amounts of feed that can be fed to animals all year long. Read on to find out more about these big, bulky storage tanks.

MIGHTY BIG MILK TANK

Bulk milk coolers are a big deal on today's dairy farm. Do you know how big? Some can hold up to 8,000 gallons of milk. A tank that big would provide enough lunch milk for 47 average-sized elementary schools for one week.

BUSHELS OF GASOLINE

Because it is a "crib" doesn't mean a corn crib is small. Large corn cribs can hold up to 2,000 bushels of corn. If all those bushels could somehow be turned into gallons of gaso-

line, there would be enough gas to drive a car around the world nearly two times.

SPRING MILK

Before bulk milk coolers were invented, farmers had to keep their milk in 5-gallon cans. Plus, they needed to keep it cold until it was taken to a dairy company. Some farmers kept their cans of milk in refrigerators, but this was very expensive. So where did farmers often choose to keep their milk? In a nearby spring, where the cold water kept the milk cool and fresh.

CEREAL GRAIN

Giant metal grain tanks found on modern farms are very important to farmers and their animals. These tanks store massive amounts of feed grain that stay fresh for a long period of time. Many of today's bulk feed storage tanks, when activated, drop the feed grain onto a conveyor which carries it into the animal feeding area. If all the feed grain from one large grain tank was made into wheat grain cereal, there would be enough to give a box to every person living in the city of Memphis, Tennessee.

SILOS

The tall, round objects found next to barns aren't old fuel tanks from the space shuttle. They're silos (sigh-lows). Silos store chopped corn stalks, called *silage*, that are fed to cows. Not all silos are tall and round. *Trench silos* are trenches in the ground filled with silage that are covered with plastic. *Bunker silos* are above ground and have wood or concrete walls with several openings. Here are a few facts about these super storage structures.

FLYING SILO?
"Air-traffic control, silo is approaching runway and is ready for take off." A flying silo? Maybe not, but they are the right size to soar. If a tall silo was laid on its side, it would be about as long as a DC-9 passenger jet.

COW CHOW-DOWN
Silos play a large role on the farm.

They hold enough silage to feed an entire herd of cattle for one year. In fact,

one large silo can hold as much as 7 million pounds of silage.

If a farmer could line up the number of cows they could feed in one day from this silo, the cow line would be almost 350 miles long. Dinner reservations would definitely be a good idea.

BATTER UP!
Step up to the plate and take a whack at hitting a ball over a silo. It would be a pretty big pop-up to hit a ball that high.

Some silos are 100 feet high, or as tall as 300 baseballs stacked on top of each other.

FILL 'ER UP!

Have you ever seen a square silo? Probably not. There is a reason why square silos aren't found on today's farms. In 1873, Fred L. Hatch, an Illinois farmer, built the first square silo above ground. When he poured the feed inside, it did not pack tightly enough because the edges were square. This allowed air to get in and spoil most of the feed. In 1882, Franklin H. King of Wisconsin built a round silo. Round silos let the feed pack together without allowing air in. Today, round silos are still being built for storing silage.

QUITTING TIME

As you can see, farm equipment plays a very important role in our lives. There are over 2 million farms in the country today. These farms take up 465 million acres of land, which covers about the area of Texas, New Mexico, Arizona, and Utah. Equipment helps produce the crops that provide us with almost all of our food, so it's easy to see why agriculture is one of the most important industries in the world.

We hope *Fun Facts About Farm Equipment* has shown you how fascinating farm equipment can be. You'll never look at these big machines the same way again!

SAFETY TIPS

A farm is a wonderful place to live and visit. But life on a farm, especially around equipment, can sometimes be dangerous. Here are some smart safety tips to keep in mind while around powerful farm machinery.

1. Tractors are not toys. They have an important job to do. Though it may look like fun, don't ever ride on tractors. There have been many incidents where extra riders have been hurt or even killed after falling off a tractor, even a tractor with a cab.

2. Never play in or on grain. Equipment used to transport and store grain on the farm has hidden dangers. Grain flowing from tanks, wagons, or trucks can pull you under and lead to suffocation.

3. Stay away from moving parts on machinery, especially chains, belts, and power take-offs (PTO's). Shields on PTO's, augers, and other farm machinery should be secure.

4. Always have adult supervision when working with farm machinery.

Because farm life involves being outdoors and around equipment, sometimes a farm can seem like a large playground. But living and working on a farm has many hazards. Farm Safety 4 Just Kids works to prevent farm-related childhood injuries, health risks, and fatalities. Contact the organization at 1-800-423-KIDS to learn more about staying safe on the farm. A healthy and safe farm is a happy farm, so always stay alert.

Order The Replica

Whether you are a serious collector or just a big fan of farm toys, you should consider a subscription to <u>The Replica</u>. This 4-color, bi-monthly magazine comes to you direct from The Ertl Company. It's full of the latest news about upcoming product releases in die cast farm toys, farm playsets, banks and other Ertl collectibles. And, from time to time, special subscriber-only, exclusive products are offered.

To receive your subscription of <u>The Replica</u>, write to:

The Ertl Company Replica Offer
Dept. 776A Highways 136 & 20
P.O. Box 500, Dyersville, IA 52040-0500

Inside the U.S.A. $10.00 for 1 year and $18.00 for 2 years
Outside the U.S.A. $14.00 for 1 year and $22.00 for 2 years

Farm Safety ♥ Just Kids

For more information on how to stay safe on the farm, call or write:

Farm Safety 4 Just Kids
110 South Chestnut Avenue
P.O. Box 458
Earlham, IA 50072

1-800-423-KIDS or 1-515-758-2827

Fun Facts About Farm Equipment was created in cooperation with Farm Safety 4 Just Kids.